Poems of the Five Mountains

Shussan Shaka by Soga Nichokuan. Detail. Shōmyōji. Kyoto.

Poems of the Five Mountains

An Introduction to the Literature of the Zen Monasteries

Marian Ury

Second, Revised Edition

Michigan Monograph Series in Japanese Studies, Number 10
Center for Japanese Studies, The University of Michigan
Ann Arbor, Michigan, 1992

Open access edition funded by the National Endowment for the Humanities/ Andrew W. Mellon Foundation Humanities Open Book Program.

© 1992 by the Center for Japanese Studies, The University of Michigan, 108 Lane Hall, Ann Arbor, MI 48109–1290

Library of Congress Cataloging in Publication Data
Ury, Marian
   Poems of the five mountains : an introduction to the literature of the Zen monasteries / by Marian Ury. — Rev. 2nd ed.
      p. cm. — (Michigan monograph series in Japanese studies ; no. 10)
      Includes bibliographical references.
      ISBN 978-0-939512-53-9 (alk. paper)
      1. Chinese poetry — Japan — Translations into English. 2. Zen poetry, Chinese — Japan — Translations into English. I. Title. II. Series.
PL 3054.5.E5U78 1992
895.1'14408 — dc20   91–32839
                                                                                      CIP

Typeset by Sans Serif, Inc., Ann Arbor, Michigan
Printed and bound by Braun-Brumfield, Inc.

A Note on the Type

This book is set in Garamond type. Jean Jannon designed it in 1615, but credit was mistakenly given to Claude Garamond (ca. 1480–1561), an early typeface designer and punch cutter, probably because it resembles his work in refining early roman fonts. It is an Old Style typeface, a group of typefaces first developed for printing and characterized by their small x-height and oblique stress.

Printed and bound by CPI Group (UK) Ltd, Croydon, CR0 4YY

ISBN 978-0-939512-53-9 (hardcover)
ISBN 978-0-472-03837-4 (paper)
ISBN 978-0-472-12815-0 (ebook)
ISBN 978-0-472-90215-6 (open access)

For Louis S. Bloom, 1896–1970
and Edith Lapin Bloom, 1899–1989

Contents

Preface to the New Edition

In the preface to the second edition of his *Seven Types of Ambiguity*, the poet and critic William Empson cites Sir Max Beerbohm's "fine reflection on revising one of his early works; he said he tried to remember how angry he would have been when he wrote it if an elderly pedant had made corrections, and how certain he would have felt that the man was wrong." I am not — I hope — a pedant at any age. On the contrary, I find myself rather less interested than I used to be in the kind of research that generates little notes about this and that, and a great deal less interested in imposing such notes on readers. I have nevertheless followed Empson's example in attempting, so far as possible, to respect the work of that earlier version of myself who produced this book; she was a better poet that I suspect I would be now, and she knew more about Zen. A very few, very minor, revisions have been made in the poems, and a page of notes has been eliminated. I have updated one or two Western-language bibliographical references. It has unfortunately not been possible to reproduce the numerous illustrations in color of the monk-poets' calligraphy that Eric Sackheim, the original publisher of the book under the Mushinsha imprint, provided for it and that were one (and perhaps the least) of the many reasons that I will always feel indebted to him. In other respects, however, the book is essentially unchanged.

I am glad to repeat the acknowledgments that appeared in the original edition. First, to the Asian Literature Program of the Asia Society under a grant from the National Endowment for the Humanities, and to the Director of the Program, Bonnie R. Crown; even now, many years later, I continue to regret the discontinuance of this program, which offered material help and encouragement to many translators. Also to Junnko T. Haverlick, David Olmsted, Delbert True, Hans Ury, and Benjamin Wallacker for various kindnesses; as well as to Cyril Birch and Burton Watson, who offered helpful suggestions and corrections on portions of the manuscript. And I should like to add to this list Bruce E. Willoughby and the University of Michigan Center for Japanese Studies.

I would be remiss if I did not add that, although my introduction speaks of this book as "only a beginning," the reader who is interested in continuing with the subject now has additional English-language sources to turn to. David Pollack's *Zen Poems of the Five Mountains* (New York: Crossroad; and Decatur, GA: Scholars Press, 1985) presents translations from a broader group of poets, the individual poems arranged and annotated to delineate the various aspects of the monks' lives and to emphasize their religious practices. A selection of *gozan* poems, translated by Burton Watson, can also be found in *From the Country of Eight Islands,* edited and translated by Hiroaki Sato and Burton Watson (Garden City, NY: Doubleday, 1981). Both volumes can be warmly recommended.

Marian Ury
June 1991

Introduction

The poems in this book were written in Chinese, in the classic *shih* form.[1] Their authors were Japanese Zen monks whose lives together span the years from 1278 to 1429, for Japan a time of turmoil but also of growth. Although ten of these sixteen men visited China, all were born and died in Japan: for all, Chinese was an acquired tongue. Most of their very many poems, and for that reason most of the poems translated here, are on subjects that have little directly to do with religion. A Buddhist monastery is a place that by its very existence magically enhances the welfare of the state; it is a place where the individual is aided to strive for enlightenment; it is simultaneously a place where men live together hierarchically in order that they may live harmoniously — a place therefore where restraint, obedience, and not least courtesy must govern the relationships among the inhabitants. Verse written in Chinese had been a medium for exchange of courtesies between men of education since education began in Japan. In secular society poems and couplets in Chinese were exchanged between friends, produced impromptu (or otherwise) at banquets, made into song-texts, used to brighten festivities and solemnize mourning. The microcosm of the Zen monastery likewise produced many occasions that called for the composition of Chinese poems: there were promotions and leave-takings, visits from friends and dignitaries of both the religious and secular spheres, sickbeds, celebrations, and anniversaries. There were filial relationships to be attended to, for the disciple by virtue of his intuition of enlightenment is accepted by his master as son and heir; his fellow disciples become his brothers, his master's teachers his ancestors, the lineage of his school the focus of his loyalty. All deserving to be honored in verse, along with such universal subjects as sorrow, old age, homesickness, and the beauty of landscapes and seasons.

The genre to which the poems in this book belong is called *gozan bungaku*. *Bungaku* means "literature"; *gozan* means "five mountains." In China and Japan monasteries were so often situated in the mountains that a mountain became synonymous with the monastery located there. Five refers not to the number of the Zen monasteries themselves but to the number of ranks in the system by which the major ones were ruled under government patronage. This system, modeled after one that existed in China under the Southern Sung, seems to have come formally into being in Japan at the beginning of the fourteenth century.[2]

The order of ranks was not fixed at first, and it was altered on a number of occasions throughout the century by command of the emperor or shogun. In 1386 there were eleven *gozan* monasteries: in descending order Kenchōji (Kamakura) and Tenryūji (Kyoto), first rank; Engakuji (Kamakura) and Shōkokuji (Kyoto), second rank; likewise Jūfukuji and Kenninji, third rank; Jōchiji and Tōfukuji, fourth rank; Jōmyōji and Manjūji, fifth rank. Superior to all was the Nanzenji in Kyoto. The criteria for rank were antiquity of origin, size, and the eminence of abbots and patrons. Lesser Zen monasteries under government patronage were assigned to the *jissetsu*, "ten chapels"; there were thirty-two of these, many in provinces distant from either the military or the imperial capital. (There were however many monasteries, including some distinguished ones, that remained outside the system.) Since the largest of the monasteries were in theory limited to 350 inhabitants, the total population of the *gozan* proper was in the neighborhood of 3,000.[3]

Zen claimed to have come to Japan in distant antiquity,[4] but Zen as a sect — that is, as lineages through which a doctrine traced by its exponents to the patriarch Bodhidharma and beyond him to Śākyamuni was inherited and handed on — first came to Japan in the last decade of the twelfth century. It was brought by Japanese pilgrims who had visited China and by Chinese missionaries, at first refugees from the Mongol government and later its emissaries.

The monasteries from which these missionaries came cultivated not only the "inner" learning, of sutras and records of Zen patriarchs, but the "outer" learning of Confucian and Taoist writings, the Histories, and poetry. One reason for this interest in secular scholarship was the need the monks felt to counter the neo-Confucian attack against Buddhism on its own ground; another was the attraction that Zen monastic life had in Sung and Yuan times for members of the educated gentry class. Many had been trained in the literary skills needed to compete in the civil service examinations but for one reason or another did not enter government service; they were men who could scarcely have conceived of leaving secular learning behind when they entered religion. Special traditions of the "outer" learning grew up within the monasteries and were inherited side by side with the religious doctrines. The ships that brought missionaries and returning pilgrims brought with them the works of Sung philosophers and late T'ang and Sung poets.

From perhaps the middle of the ninth century until the time of these Zen pilgrims, Japan had almost no contact with the living cultural tradition of China; Chinese learning, despite its prestige, was the possession of a few court families that handed down the dusty heirloom unaltered from generation to generation. Though the Zen monks' understanding of the new continental philosophy might be superficial,[5] the fact that they were acquainted with it gave them glamour in the eyes of emperors and, especially, of military dictators eager to confirm their cultural qualifications to rule; drawing close to influential patrons by this means, the monks could turn the conversation to the doctrines of their school. Facility as belle-lettrists made the monks pleasing companions. The means came to overwhelm the end. As is well known, by 1600, the time of the founding of the Tokugawa shogunate, in some monasteries Confucianism was studied to the exclusion of religion. From 1299 on, when the first missionary actively to instruct his Japanese disciples in secular learning arrived, for a little over a century, men who were both Zen monks and poets apologized to themselves for their infatuation with Chinese verse. It was permissible, they said, to compose Chinese verse as long as it did not become a preoccupation that replaced religious striving; or it was permissible because the Buddhas and patriarchs had given voice to their enlightenment in verse — although where secular verse is concerned this is surely begging the question. Or they simply forbade it to their disciples while practicing it themselves. The warnings were not heeded for long: by the middle of the fifteenth century, according to the testimony of the polymath Ichijō Kaneyoshi,[6] the *gozan* monks had turned into Confucian belle-lettrists in monks' clothing. In the fourteenth century there existed a creative tension between the religious vocation and the seductions of secular poetry. A guilty conscience need by no means be a bad thing for art. It is generally conceded that *gozan* poetry of the fourteenth century excels that of later times; afterward, poems became nothing more than display pieces for the monks' learning.[7]

How good is the poetry at its best?

As regards language, we learn that only two or three of the poets, notably Zekkai and Chūgan, were so fluent that they could think in Chinese, but perhaps this is not so very important, for Chinese poems are written in a language of their own, very different from the spoken or even from most kinds of written prose. From time to time the monks would discover to their pride that their poems had been praised in China as being not recognizable as the work of foreigners — but this is scarcely conclusive, as it betrays an opposite expectation.

As a whole, Chinese verses, *kanshi,* written in Japan are taxed by critics with lacking originality and immediacy. It is true that cultural colonials rarely dare to be innovative. But the assumption that writing in a foreign tongue made it difficult for the Japanese to deal appropriately with native subjects is, I think, not quite true or fair. My selection of poems includes a number that describe the Japanese landscape. They do it rather strangely: the poet quotes tags from the classics, reshuffles lines from T'ang poets, and cites bits of Taoist lore in the act of expressing a love for his land and a pride in it that is entirely Japanese. The stylistic garb that he assumes, though in its essence ultimately foreign, is not exotic; long acquaintance has made it too familiar for that. It may be relevant to this argument that although a number of the poets translated here wrote sermons in Japanese, none wrote poems in Japanese. None doubted the adequacy of Chinese as a poetic medium. And surely, given the formal limitations of the Japanese *waka*, no other language than Chinese could have described the wonder and sorrow of the monks' experience of China itself.

One specific criticism made of *kanshi* is that the Japanese were more skilled at producing fine couplets than complete poems.[8] I think this stricture justified, although not invariably; Zekkai in particular is exempt from it. It accounts, however, for the preponderance in this volume of four-line poems rather than eight; the briefer form concentrates the energy of the poem.

A note regarding the style of the translation: I have generally preferred a slightly elevated over an informal tone in my renderings because it seemed suited to these authors' conception of their dignity as poets. Each line of the English represents a line of the original. Beyond that I have no special convictions on the art of translation, at least none worth expounding, except the observation that, like politics, translation is the art of the possible. One tries to be honest and at the same time wants one's children to behave well in public. This translation was begun and continued out of pleasure — pleasure partly in the act of discovery, but pleasure also in the poems themselves, whatever their faults, and I hope my readers will share it with me. These poems represent only a very small portion of what can be found within *gozan bungaku:* this book is only a beginning.

Finally, regarding personal names: all of the authors of the poems have double names, each half written with two characters. The second half is the *hōmyō*, or religious name, the taboo personal name equivalent to the *jitsumyō* of the layman. The first half is his literary name (*go* or *ji*) or rather one of them, since most poet-monks had several. Japanese writers are not consistent in their usage, but to make things less confusing for the reader I cite poets always by the double name or by the first part of the name alone.

NOTES

[1] There is evidence that the *gozan* monks were familiar as readers with poems in the *tz'u* form, but they only rarely composed in it themselves; this is the conclusion of Kanda Kiichiro in his *Nihon ni okeru Chūgoku Bungaku* 1 (1965), 16–60.

[2] For a detailed study of the medieval Japanese Zen monastic system and discussion of the place within it of Chinese learning, see Martin Collcutt, *Five Mountains: The Rinzai Zen Monastic Institution in Medieval Japan* (Cambridge, MA: Council on East Asian Studies, Harvard University, 1981).

[3] Monasteries within the system were of the Rinzai sect; those outside it were mainly Sōtō, although there were exceptions. A system of rotation of high-ranking positions within the *gozan* monasteries was supposed to insure that no one lineage group dominated a monastery.

[4] A legend that appears in the *Nihongi* (720) but may be found, for example, in the *Nihon Ryōiki* (ca. 822) and even in *The Tale of Genji* tells how Prince Shōtoku encountered a starving man at Kataoka and gave him his robe. The starving man died but vanished from his grave, in the manner of a Chinese immortal. See W. G. Aston, *Nihongi* (Tokyo, 1972 [reprint]), 2:144–45. The Zen monks came to identify the starving man with their patriarch Bodhidharma; their version of the story appears in, for example, *Genkō Shakusho* (1322), ch. 1:1.

[5] See Wajima Yoshio, *Chūsei no Jugaku* (1965).

[6] Quoted in Tsuji Zennosuke, *Nihon Bukkyō Shi* 4 (1964), 447.

[7] This is the judgment of Tamamura Takeji, *Gozan Bungaku* (1966). Tsuji dates the decline of *gozan* poetry from the death in 1488 of Son'an Reigen, the last of the poets represented in a contemporary anthology of quatrains (*chüeh-chü*) called the *Kajōshū* (*Zoku Gunsho Ruijū* doc. 320). Poems came to be written chiefly to flatter patrons — a motive by no means unknown at earlier times; around 1520 there was a further decline into homosexual love poems addressed to young boys. Tsuji (op. cit., see esp. 438, 450) characterizes these as "repulsive."

On the subject of the "guilty conscience," see William R. LaFleur, *The Karma of Words: Buddhism and the Literary Arts in Medieval Japan* (Berkeley: University of California Press, 1983).

This book ignores one important fifteenth-century figure. Ikkyū Sōjun's verse was less skilled than that of the academics but marked by his vigorous and original personality. A short description of his life and work, together with a translation of some poems, appears in Donald Keene's *Landscapes and Portraits* (Tokyo and Palo Alto, 1971), 226–41. A full-length study is Sonja Arntzen's *Ikkyū and the Crazy Cloud Anthology: A Zen Poet of Medieval Japan* (Tokyo: University of Tokyo Press, 1986).

It should be remembered that Ikkyū stands apart from his sect and time.

[8] The reader who wishes to pursue these criticisms should consult a brief but illuminating article by Burton Watson, "Some Remarks on the *Kanshi*," in *Journal-Newsletter of the Association of Teachers of Japanese* 5.2 (July 1968), 15–21.

Kokan Shiren

Gozan bungaku bifurcates into two traditions, the poetic and the scholarly. The second of these, which came to be dominant from the fifteenth century on, traced its founding to Kokan Shiren (1278–1346). Initiated into the tradition of Chinese studies handed down at the Japanese court since the eighth century by the descendants of Sugawara Michizane and Kibi no Mabi, conversant with the newer currents from the continent, passionately partisan in rehearsing Chinese literary controversies of bygone centuries, convinced that Japan was the destined true home of both Buddhism and Chinese civilization, Kokan wrote voluminously. His magnum opus, *Genkō Shakusho* completed and presented to the throne in 1322, is the first comprehensive history of Buddhism in Japan. The ambitious author modeled it, by his own claim, on Chinese collections of biographies of eminent monks and on the classics of Confucian history. (It is possible, however, that he had a nearer model in *Fo-tsu T'ung-chi,* a history of the T'ien-t'ai school, compiled 1258–69.) Among his other works were a treatise on the causes of illness, polemics asserting the superiority of Zen over other Buddhist schools, a collection of the discourses of the founder of his lineage, Enni Ben'en (Enni [1202–80] had won a debate with a Confucian opponent by challenging him to show the genealogy through which he had inherited his doctrine from Confucius), the first important commentary on the Laṅkāvatāra sutra by a Japanese, works for the instruction of students that included a handbook of phrases from the Confucian classics to be quoted when writing the parallel prose compositions fashionable in Zen monasteries, and the first Chinese rhyming dictionary written expressly for use by Japanese. By 1554 this dictionary had gone through ten known printings, a measure of the popularity of Chinese versifying in Japan.

Mild-mannered and unassertive among his fellows, always in delicate health, Kokan as a young man was kept from going to China by his mother. In Kamakura, however, he was able to study with a master sent from China in 1299, Issan Ichinei (I-shan I-ning, 1244–1317). Issan was learned not only in religion but in belles lettres, painting, calligraphy, and mathematics; he was of course unable to communicate orally with his Japanese students but instructed them by means of writing. Because Issan's teaching stimulated so many of the first generation of poets represented here, historians account him the true ancestor of *gozan bungaku*. The literary taste he transmitted, however, was not that of the monasteries in contemporary China but represented the latter half of the Sung dynasty.

Judgment of Kokan's works has been clouded by the ill will of adherents of rival Zen lineages. Issan's was the first important voice to come from China after the attempted invasions of Japan by the Mongols under Khubilai in 1274 and 1281; as travel to and from the continent increased and the Japanese acquired up-to-date knowledge about literary styles in China, the poems of his pupil Kokan would soon come to seem hopelessly old-fashioned. They had few of the brilliant couplets the Japanese were so fond of, were called unrefined in language and deficient in technique. Some modern critics continue these complaints, but by no means all do. Kokan's best poems show a strength of imagination that should particularly recommend them to modern readers.

Dawn

A frosty bell echoes the fifth watch;
The colors of dawn are still invisible;
Behind my house, in the treetops
Two or three wakeful crows, cawing.

The night was divided into five watches of approximately two modern hours each. The two-hour period before and after midnight was the third watch, from three to five a.m., the fifth watch. The scene is early winter.

3

The Earthquake

That which was fixed, moves; the hard becomes soft.
The earth is like waves, my house like a boat.
A time of dread, but also of charm:
Wind bells chime without rest, though there's no wind.

Foam

The angry waves have set their footprints in sand-hollows;
Flowers falling do not fade, and snow does not melt;
The ever-existing Dharma-body of Buddha is changeless;
In the gardens of the mirage-born city grow plantains.

Well-known passages in the *Vimalakīrtinirdeśa* sutra liken the body to a plantain
or banana-plant because of its hollowness, and to a bubble of foam; the elements
of phenomenal existence that give rise to the illusion of selfhood to a city created
by magic in the air. Zen teaches that in enlightenment is realized the identity
between phenomena, in their essential evanescence, and the changeless
noumenon.

Rain

I've heard that Sāgara's rain, like truth,
Delights each heaven in different shape,
And now here's proof: I watch the rain
Stamp rings on water, shower jewels on lilies.

Mahayana Buddhism holds that the Buddha varied his teaching of the Dharma to suit the differing abilities of his hearers, just as the rain falls on all plants alike yet nourishes each according to its ability to grow. The heavens of the poem are the six heavens of the Realm of Desire, in which, in Buddhist mythology, the ancient gods of India reside; Sāgara, whose name means Ocean, is a dragon-king.

Nāgārjuna

The Dharma-jewels of the Tathāgata were scattered like ashes;
Who among the throng would chieftain the ministers?
He examined the merest mustard-grains in the palm of his
    hand;
With his vajra key at a single blow he opened the gate.

Early Zen in Japan, particularly as cultivated in the *gozan* monasteries, had strong affinities with the Esoteric teachings of Shingon and Tendai Buddhism. This is the first of a series of eight poems by Kokan celebrating Esoteric patriarchs. There is a tradition in Esoteric Buddhism that Śākyamuni predicted that eight hundred years after his own extinction Nāgārjuna would appear. Mustard grains, because of their hardness and bitterness, are used in Esoteric rites to symbolize the wisdom that subdues the realm of Māra; according to legend, Nāgārjuna performed such a rite, whereupon the gates of an iron stupa opened, disclosing the bodhisattva Vajrasattva, who conferred the Esoteric initiation on him. The gate in line 4 is both the gate of the stupa and, metaphorically, the gate of enlightenment.

The Mosquito

The point of its beak is as sharp as an awl,
With a roar as of thunder it circles my bed;
Should the frail partition of gauze be pierced once — why
An iron-ox hide would fester to muck!

A Spring View

With warm winds and long days the hundred living things
    revive —
Alone, I'm ashamed of my fusty self before Spring's radiant
    newness.
Water blurs into sky, both gem-green;
Blossoms hide the trees, all garish red and crimson!
Pleasure-wagons, sightseers' horses, rush to be first;
Dancing swallows, wheeling warblers, frolic to their hearts'
    content.
Most charming of all, there's a haze-distant village
And wrapped in its smoke, the thousandfold ranks of willows.

A Village by the River

The river village lies pale by the swollen waters,
The sand stamped criss-cross with antique symbols, the
    footprints of birds.
A white-haired angler sits in solitude, pole in hand;
Ducks in pairs wet their bellies on the wave-crests.
Snub-nosed skiffs rock at anchor before the breeze;
A skinny cow with bowed horns leads her calf.
Beyond reed banks and rush-grown coves, over thatched
    rooftops,
Round, begins the sun. A rich smoke rises from the hearths.

Winter Moon

A mountain grove, leafless —
Cloudless skies, wind still —
Dawn colors pinch the frost; chill moonlight overflows;
All heaven and earth should bear the name-board "Palace of
   Broad Cold."

The "Palace of Broad Cold" is the palace in the moon.

Sesson Yūbai

Sesson Yūbai (b. 1290; not to be confused with the painter Sesson Shūkei, b. 1504) was a dharma-disciple (that is, religious heir) as well as secular pupil of Issan Ichinei. What Kokan was to the tradition of scholarship within *gozan bungaku* Sesson was to its poetry. The two men were friends — Sesson called on Kokan several times during the latter's last illness — but were almost opposites in temperament and career. In 1306, at an age at which the handsome Kokan had been employed in chanting mantras at the court of Ex-Emperor Kameyama, Sesson boarded a merchant ship for China. There Issan's recommendation secured him a warm reception and discipleship under Issan's own dharma-brother. As a precociously gifted young foreigner, Sesson was made much of, and his well-wishers included the painter Ch'ao Meng-fu. In 1308 there came to the Chinese throne a new emperor who wished to avenge the humiliation of his grandfather Khubilai by the Japanese. Among the measures he took was imprisoning all the Japanese monks in China. Sesson was suspected of spying and barely escaped execution; his Chinese master died. Released from his jail in Hu-chou, he was exiled north to Ch'ang-an; after three years he was further exiled to the far west, beyond Han-ku Pass. There he remained for ten years, immersing himself in the study of the Confucian classics and the *Chuang Tzu,* which he had loved since boyhood. When at length a pardon allowed him back in Ch'ang-an, he was prevented from returning home to Japan by the Yuan court, this time through the bestowal of honors: he was given the abbacy of a temple and the title of Meditation Master (Ch'an-shih, Zenji). Sesson returned to Japan in 1329. He had lived in China for so long and from such an early age that he had become as much Chinese as Japanese.

Sesson's later career in Japan is typical of that of many eminent clerics of his time, periods of seclusion and semiretirement alternating with abbacies assumed reluctantly at imperial order. His bearing was severe; it was said that he had never once been seen to smile. On the twenty-sixth of the eleventh month of 1246 he suffered a stroke while performing memorial services for one of Issan's attendants and could no longer move his right arm. On the second day of the twelfth month he attempted to write his deathbed poem using his left arm but was unable to make the brush strokes; in a fit of temper he threw the brush over the screen. But it is recorded that he died peacefully.

Sesson's poems convey something of his forthright character. While the other *gozan* poets preferred to write *lü-shih* ("regulated verse"), a strict form that prescribes parallelism in ways that can be both constricting and supportive, Sesson excelled at the freer *ku-shih* ("ancient verse").

Chance Verses

I, monk, am exiled west of Han-ku Pass,
Yellow hide, starved belly, bones jut out like crags —
In season I'll sit to banquet amid dark rocks and boulders:
I lack only the Preacher of Emptiness to make my friend.

. . . . .

I, monk, am exiled west of Han-ku Pass,
A single wisteria branch my companion.
South Mountain's green joins Mount Sung with Mount Hua:
This one ascent cheers a whole life's sufferings.

While traveling westward into exile Sesson composed ten verses each with the same opening line. The Preacher of Emptiness was Subhūti, the one among the Buddha's disciples who best understood this metaphysical principle that is the foundation of Zen teaching. Both South Mountain (Nan-shan) and Hua-shan are in Shensi; Nan-shan is a spur of the K'un-lun Mountains, extending to Sung-shan in Honan.

Composed on the First Day of the Seventh Month, the Beginning of Autumn

Heaven and earth so slight: I too, a transient guest
Through the scurrying months and years, endure alarms.
Leaves under *wu-t'ung* trees bring news of autumn;
Wind over water-weed bids farewell to warmth.
On Min-shan's peaks I see only the color of cold snow;
Not yet on the river has the waves' sound grown calm.
Where shall I moor my boat? Crickets shrilly cry.
At dusk blue mountain pavilions press against the clearing
   sky.

This poem was written while Sesson was traveling up the Min River from Ch'eng-tu, his place of exile.

Yearning for My Friend on an Autumn Night

I'm by origin a man of the southeast,
And I constantly long for a guest from the southeast;
How will this splendid evening be endured?
Deserted, the rural walks by the city wall.
Dew lies on the chrysanthemums, permeates the garden;
Wind rustles the branches, flutters the drifting leaves.
I hum to myself, but you, dear friend, do not come,
And the bright moon shines in vain in an empty sky.

This poem was composed when the poet was living in a monastery outside the walls of Ch'ang-an; the "southeast" is Japan.

Irregular Verse

I take no joy in other people's praise,
Other people's slander doesn't scare me,
Just because my ties with the world are sparse
The heart in my bosom is unconstrained as water.
Bound in prison fetters, I survived,
And stayed on in Ch'ang-an three years —
When sometimes it suits my mood to sing
I speak out straight: why bother with fancy words?

Irregular Verse

I'm not T'ao Ch'ien:
It's the northern window I love to look from —
It's not because it was Fu Hsi's custom
That on impulse I take up new verses.
There are brushes eternally ready to copy for hire,
In antiquity withered, today half-consumed by worms.
If you yourself have talent that can stand on its own
It's no use being earnest about petty things.

Line 2 has "northern window" to contrast with the eastern window of one of the most famous poems of the beloved Six Dynasties poet-recluse T'ao Ch'ien. Fu Hsi was the first of the legendary Five Emperors who taught mankind the arts of civilization.

There Is No Resting

Who travels the Way heeds the Heart's and the Way's
    beginnings,
But the Way's everywhere, without boundaries —
I'll go till the rivers run dry, exhaust the peaks:
In the calm of the clouds I'll sit, and watch the moon light up
    the heavens.

Like many of the other Zen literati, Sesson was learned in the literature of
philosophical Taoism. Way, *tao,* is a Buddhist as well as Taoist term, and he
"who travels the Way" (literally, man of the Way) can be either a Taoist adept or
a Buddhist monk. *Tao* is used as a synonym for *bodhi,* enlightenment, and line 2
can be read as a description of the freedom of the mind that has realized its true
state. The third line might be paraphrased "I'll go to the ends of the earth" —
but, additionally, it may allude to the association of mountain peaks with the
cult of immortality in Taoism. The moon is a Buddhist metaphor for
enlightenment.

Autumn's Whiteness

Autumn gales drive the shimmering silver saucer of the moon;
Its reflection falls on the clear river, cold as a great length of
   glossy silk.
Even if red flowers of waterwort were added to these banks
For the man of the Way there is only perception of the
   one-color realm.

In Zen teaching "one-color realm" denotes a state of awareness, gained in medi-
tation, in which the notion of the distinctness of phenomena from phenomena
and from the noumenon is destroyed. According to Chinese cosmology, there are
correspondences between seasons of the year, colors, directions, etc.; the color
corresponding to autumn is white.

Thinking of the Old Man of Precious Cloud

On rain-rinsed mountains the colors of autumn linger;
Soon pines turn aged under snow: shapes of the year's chill.
May my noble master be safe beyond the wide ocean —
Where he grasped the broom to preach my mind sees an
    empty hall.

Old Man of Precious Cloud was a sobriquet of Issan, who died while Sesson was
in China. The broom is the scepter of authority held by the preacher in Zen
monasteries.

Jakushitsu Genkō

Jakushitsu Genkō (1290–1367) was a pupil of Issan, though like Kokan not his dharma-disciple. Jakushitsu studied in China from 1320 to 1326. After his return to Japan he founded a temple in Bingo Province and spent twenty-five years in the area of modern Okayama Prefecture, refusing summonses from both the shogunate and the imperial court. His fame was such that great numbers of eminent monk-disciples came to him in his mountain retreat.

Double Yang

Braving the dawn to sweep leaves I stand by my garden's
   edge —
Westwind blows through the reed fence; dew soaks my hem.
Just now a mountain child comes to pluck chrysanthemums —
He says to me: "Today is Double Yang!"

In Chinese science the number nine represents the ascendancy of *yang* and is
called Greater Yang; accordingly the ninth day of the ninth month is known as
Double Yang Day. On this day it was customary in both ancient China and Japan
to drink a millet wine infused with chrysanthemum leaves and petals in order to
ward off evil influences and obtain long life. In Japan, where this day provided
the occasion for one of the five great festivals celebrated annually at court, there
were many other observances involving chrysanthemums — chrysanthemum con-
tests, chrysanthemum poem contests, etc. Alone in his hermitage the poet must
be reminded what day it is.

Living in the Mountains

I don't crave fame and profit or care that I'm poor;
Hiding in the depths of the mountains I keep far away the
    world's dust;
The year has waned and the skies are cold: who'd be my
    companion?
The plum blossoms are adorned in moonlight — one branch,
    new.

Counsel for the Congregation of Monks

To train in meditation you must be truly stalwart,
Make all your body and mind as hard as steel —
Look well at the Buddhas and patriarchs of former times:
Was any among them a trifler at his ease?

Events of a Cold Night

Wind disorders the cold forest, bright under frost-moon;
A guest comes: lofty talk past the Middle Watch.
Chopsticks laid on the hearth-rim and roasting yams
    forgotten:
Through the stillness I hear on the windows the rain taps of
    falling leaves.

Ryūsen Reisai

Ryūsen Reisai (d. 1365) was from childhood on a favorite disciple of Kokan and companion to him on his travels through Japan. After the master's death, Ryūsen became head of the cloister Kokan had established; his last years were devoted to efforts, ultimately successful, to have *Genkō Shakusho* entered into the officially recognized Buddhist canon. Ryūsen's father was the Emperor Go-Daigo, his mother an imperial concubine who was given in marriage to a member of the Minamoto clan shortly before the infant's birth. Go-Daigo's ambition to restore to the reigning emperor authority that had vanished centuries before precipitated sixty years of civil war. Poetic laments over the destruction wrought by war and time are often perfunctory, but Ryūsen's are not.

Cold Rain

Soon it will turn to snow. The chill will come, not
   blossoms —
A pattering drizzle that matches the traveler's grief.
Heard by all alike, rain dripping from the eaves,
But to him who sorrows a sound that breaks the heart.

The third line plays upon the same parable as that of Kokan's "Rain," above.

Inscribed on the Wall of an Old Temple

Dead leaves reel on the wind through vacant passageways,
Autumn insects chirping climb the painted hall,
Even the "Drooping Millet" verse of the *Book of Odes*
Can't teach a man's heart to be iron or harden his guts to
    stone.

"There was the millet with its drooping heads. . . . "; the poem referred to in line
3 is traditionally thought a lament on the desolation of the ancient capital of
Chou. See James Legge, *The Chinese Classics*, vol. 4 (Oxford: Oxford University
Press, 1935), 110–11.

Evening Light

The setting sun's half-circle fades in a corner of the peaks;
Its rays glint upward into tangled forest;
The sky in its vastness is spread with crimson silk
For a sketch in pale ink: crows flying homeward.

On the Road on a Spring Day

There is no coming, there is no going.
From what quarter departed? Toward what quarter bound?
Pity him! in the midst of his journey, journeying —
Flowers and willows in spring profusion, everywhere fragrance.

The poem begins with a Zen truism, which is expanded into a personal statement.

Musings While on the Road

I think of those who came and went on this same road in
    former years —
How many have gone home to earth, while I remain, useless
    and alone.
On these rocks, in the shadow of these trees abides my mortal
    love:
Whom have I taught who will one day grieve in his turn to
    part from them?

Betsugen Enshi

Betsugen Enshi (1295–1364) studied in China from 1319 to 1329, returning in the company of Jikusen Bonsen (Chu-hsien Fan-hsien, 1293–1349), a Chinese master around whom gathered such men as Sesson Yūbai and Chūgan Engetsu. (Several members of Jikusen's large entourage, including a Chinese disciple of one of the men sent from Japan to invite him and a Japanese disciple of Jikusen's teacher, were in the boat in which Sesson returned.) Where Sesson's outlook on literature was the conservative one he had acquired from Issan, tempered with his own firsthand experience of the continent, Jikusen brought with him the latest literary fashions from the Chinese monasteries. Most marked among these was the increasing preference toward exclusively secular subject matter; some monks, though not all, soon came to look down on the work of the earlier poets as embarrassingly churchly.

Betsugen was one of the few *gozan* masters who belonged to a Sōtō lineage. He earned distinction as a preacher as well as a poet.

Brewing Tea

Green clouds spiral and twine, are drawn into the wind in a
    long stream;
On my cup's surface the faces of white foam-flowers are cool.
The mountain moon comes into my window; plum-tree
    shadows move;
Pouring again and again into my unglazed cup I sip the
    lingering fragrance.

Sitting in Meditation

My mountain dwelling is dark all day in the rain
While plums are half yellow-ripe, half still green.
One bench in a lonely room — Always I'm in *samadhi*,
Forbidden to watch the flowers and birds come to my garden.

In the form of meditation taught by the Zen school the eyes must be kept half-closed.

Things Seen and Heard

The rain has stopped; on the pond there open white lotus
    flowers;
With the dew I come to pluck them and put them in a
    bronze vase.
In the pure summer breeze I pillow my head under the north
    window —
From the trees at noon cicadas' voices resound into my
    dreams.

Flowers in vases are used as offerings to the Buddha.

An Evening View on the River

A lonely boat, short-oared, skitters away —
Voices come hushed and sad to the shores as the sun sets;
North of the River and south of the River, from the willow
    banks
Wind-fluttered wine-shop pennants' reflections flow into the
    sky.

This poem was written in China; the River is the Yangtze. Wine shops displayed red banners with a design of ascending and descending dragons.

39

Sitting at Night

The course of each man's life is ordained by Heaven before his
    birth:
Do poverty or riches, success or failure in office come by
    chance?
I count back one by one through the many days and months
To recall my distant wanderings among ancient mountains
    and rivers.
In the autumn wind: "white hair — three thousand *chang*
    long!"
In the evening rain: blue lamplight — fifty years!
As I lean against the wall and muse upon times now long
    gone by
With a single cry the first wild goose of autumn crosses the
    cold heavens.

The fifth line quotes from a celebrated verse by Li Po, one of seventeen that the
T'ang poet composed at a place called Ch'iu-p'u ("Autumn Bay"):

    White hair — three thousand *chang* long!
    My hair has grown so long because of grief.
    Yet I don't understand the image in the mirror —
    Where did it get its autumn frost?

A *chang* was equal to about ten feet; the charm — and for most Western readers
the weakness — of the original lies in its hyperbole. "Sitting at Night" is one of
the poems Betsugen Enshi wrote in Japan.

Chūgan Engetsu

Chūgan Engetsu (1300–75) began life as an unwanted child, cared for by a wet nurse and the paternal grandmother who in his eighth year (about six and a half by Western count) entered him in the Jūfukuji as a temple boy. He began the study of the Confucian classics not many years after. In religion he studied Esoteric Buddhism as well as both Rinzai and Sōtō Zen. Among the masters impressed by his youthful reputation as a scholar was Kokan, who received him at a time when, busy completing his history, he had closed his door to almost all other callers; Kokan even let him see a draft of his work. In his nineteenth year, Chūgan went to Hakata in Kyushu with the aim of embarking for China, but he was refused permission to leave by the local government authorities. In 1324 he at last made the voyage; he returned in 1332. A lonely idealist whose adherence to what he considered right made him the object of factional rancor, in 1344 Chūgan attempted unsuccessfully to go to China once more. His motive may have been the hope of escaping the unpleasantness that surrounded him despite his enjoyment of the patronage of a powerful military family, the Ōtomo.

It was the custom for a man's biographical annals to be prepared by disciples after his death; Chūgan, however, insisted on writing his own. Among his writings was a history of Japan called the *Nihon Sho*, which argued that the Japanese imperial house was descended from Wu T'ai-po, eldest son of the Duke of Chou of Chinese classical times but set aside by the Duke as heir; the book was suppressed by order of the imperial court, and no copy survives.

Musing on Antiquity at Chin-lu

Its great men pass on without cease, but the land is
    uncrushed, ungentled;
The Six Courts have crumbled utterly, but "the mountains
    and rivers abide."
The ancient sites of royal offices: merchants' and fishermen's
    dwellings;
The sounds that lingered from precious groves: woodsmen's
    and oxherds' songs.
The canyons are filled with endless clouds, constantly bearing
    rain;
On the Great River the winds are calmed, but waves still
    arise.
The fair beauties of those years — where are they now?
For the traveler from afar, in this vast view, how much to
    admire and to mourn!

Chin-lu, modern Nanking, had been a royal city during much of the Six Dynas-
ties period. Line 2 contains a quotation from what is perhaps Tu Fu's best known
poem. "Precious groves," literally trees of jade or jewel-trees, is a common meta-
phor for men of superior pure demeanor. The "Great River" is the Yangtze.

Stopping at Hakata upon My Return to My Native Land I Sent Two Poems to Betsugen Enshi

I

I think of the past, when together we roamed the rivers and
   lakes, rootless as duckweed;
Each floating with the current was borne eastward home across
   the sea.
What together and apart we cherish has no limit —
Isn't it just what exists in wordlessness?

II

Lord of White Cloud Hall, our white-haired master —
Of his followers in the Hall, who has white eyebrows, mark of
   excellence?
Older and younger brothers, when you meet for pleasure,
   when you talk,
Do not forget the young wanderer who once came to you for
   his gruel.

Betsugen Enshi, who had returned to Japan only a few years before Chūgan, was dharma-disciple of Tōmin (or Tōmyō) E'nichi (T'ung-ming Hui-jih), a teacher from China whose residence in the Engakuji in Kamakura was known as White Cloud Hall. Tōmin, unlike almost all other important figures within the *gozan,* belonged to a Sōtō lineage, but Chūgan, though formally a member of a Rinzai lineage and therefore an outsider, served and studied under him for more than twenty years, from the age of sixteen. The second of these two poems is an elaborate compliment to Tōmin and his congregation of monks. The monks never fully accepted Chūgan, and estrangement from fellows and master was to darken his last days.

At Kamado-ga-seki

Mountains guard the sea; in the harbor a thousand masts —
Smoke from thick-clustered habitation hides the late sun.
"Ea-yaw" — oar sounds part the darkening mist:
Startled white herons fly across the broad blue water.

In 1333, the year following his arrival at Hakata upon his return from China, Chūgan journeyed to Kyoto. His ship took him around the northern tip of Kyushu and through the Inland Sea along the coast of Honshu, landing finally at Hyōgo. This poem and the two that follow are from a series of ten describing the notable sights encountered en route. Kamado-ga-seki (Nagashima, near the southeast corner of modern Yamaguchi Prefecture) was famous since antiquity as a port. The name, which might be translated "Cook-Stove Straits," is obviously the inspiration for the second line.

At Itsukushima

Excellent landscape of divine sport, where the holy traces are
manifested:
Mountain peaks of a yonder world in the midst of the
frothing sea!
The moon shines on the winding corridors; and the tide is
full —
In the deep of night who is here in these crystal mansions?

The island of Itsukushima is still one of the most renowned sights in Japan, a
focus for pilgrimages since the seventh century, when the Shinto shrine was
established. The shrine, with its long open corridors, extends some 160 meters
into the sea; at high tide its *torii* (ritual gates) seem to be floating on the surface
of the water. The shrine had special associations with the Taira clan, defeated in
1185 at Dan-no-ura, another place that Chūgan visited and wrote about on this
voyage. Taoist, Buddhist, and Shinto beliefs mingle in this poem. "Holy traces"
denotes the Shinto gods who inhabit the shrine; according to Shinto-Buddhist
syncretic notions, Shinto deities are the "manifest traces" of the Buddhas. In
Taoist legend three islands of the immortals rise in the shape of mountains peaks
from the ocean. Early Japanese legends, most likely influenced by Taoist beliefs,
tell of a dragon-king's mansion under the sea; a second poem on Itsukushima by
Chūgan speaks of it explicitly.

At Tomo Harbor

Cold wind in the southern trees: autumn in the city by the
    sea;
The smoke of war-fires vanished but the ashes not yet cleared
    away —
Singing girls, knowing nothing of the destruction of the state,
Clamor and clang forth their tunes as they sail upon orchid
    boats.

Early in 1332, Emperor Go-Daigo, deposed for plotting against the Hōjō lords of
the Kamakura shogunate, was exiled to Oki. He escaped and returned to Kyoto
in the summer of 1333, a few months before Chūgan's poem was written. The
period of civil war inaugurated was to last almost to the end of the century. Both
this poem and the next play upon a quatrain, by the T'ang poet Tu Mu, included
in *San-t'i Shih*, an anthology newly introduced and much admired by the *gozan*
literati:

> Stopping for the Night at Ch'in-huai
> Mist envelops the cold waters, moonlight envelops the sand —
> At night my boat rests at Ch'in-huai, close by the wine shops.
> Dancing girls, knowing nothing of the sorrows of the destruction of the state,
> On the far bank of the river still sing "Flowers in the Rear Garden."

"Flowers in the Rear Garden" was the name of a tune by the last emperor of the
Ch'en dynasty, Ch'en Shu-pao (553–604), who — as tradition has it — gave him-
self up to debauchery. Ch'in-huai was his capital.

Tomo was an important stopping place for ships that traveled along the Inland
Sea, and Chūgan was not the only traveler to take note of its many female
entertainers. Thirty years earlier the author of *Towazugatari*, on pilgrimage to
Itsukushima, called at Tomo and observed a religious colony composed of former
prostitutes (Karen Brazell, trans., *The Confessions of Lady Nijō* [Garden City,
NY: Anchor Books, 1973], 228).

A Chance Verse: Sorrowing for the Past

This day last year Kamakura was destroyed —
Its splendid views, its temples all are gone.
Peddler girls, knowing nothing of the bitterness of the monks,
Hawk firewood and greens down former official lanes.

In the fifth month of 1333 the forces of Nitta Yoshisada, fighting on behalf of
Go-Daigo, defeated the Hōjō and burned Kamakura to the ground.

In Tu Mu's original poem the expression *shang nü* was used to denote female
entertainers. Chūgan uses the same characters here, but for their literal meaning
of "merchant women"; in "At Tomo Harbor" he had imitated the meaning of Tu
Mu's phrase but used different characters.

This is the first of seven laments on various subjects that Chūgan composed
under this title.

Atami

Dreams crumble at midnight; that echoing roar
Is the boiling of the waters at the base of the cliff.
Flumes divide the springs from their source; steam envelops
  the houses —
Each dwelling provides baths; there guests rent chambers.
By the shore the earth is warm; in winter there is no snow —
Over mountain roads the sky is cold; at dawn I tread on frost.
A distant island: rain. Black clouds and mist.
A red tide bids farewell to the moon as it falls into dimness.

Atami, now a popular resort, was known from the time of the earliest histories
for its radioactive hot springs, many of which discharge under the sea.

In the Evening of the Year

In the evening of the year, under chilly skies
When the wind is pure and the moon is white
I chant leisurely verses, playing the elegant hermit —
But sitting alone I sigh over dim shapes,
Unable to explain the world's workings
Except that each life of itself has a limit:
   If I can only divert the present moment
   I'll not need to think of the time when this self has ended.

Mugan Sō-ō

Mugan Sō-ō, compared by admirers to Chūgan for the breadth of his learning, never went to China. After training as a youth in the Tōfukuji in Kyoto, he returned to his native village in Izumo Province and remained there for twenty years. His later years were spent in the Tōfukuji. The date of his birth is unknown; he died in 1374.

Description of Things Seen on the Sixth Day of the Second Month

Waking from noontime sleep I open my bamboo fan —
Spring clouds, spring water already brilliant in the sunset.
Whose son is he who comes riding along the shore
And startles the herons and gulls from the sand into flight?

Shizan Myōzai

Shizan Myōzai (1296–1377) was dharma-disciple to Musō Sōse-
ki's master Bukkoku Zenji. He visited China (the dates of his
journey are unknown) and after his return was for a time abbot
of the Tenryūji.

My Friends
Returning to Their Homes

When we said goodbye at the bridge where the rivers meet
Autumn winds parted our sleeves. Some of us went west,
    some east.
Next morning, as you journeyed to your home temples,
I remember the whimpering of the monkeys, cold under the
    moon.

The bridge in line 1 was in the valley near the Kuo-ch'ing-ssu on Mount T'ien-t'ai. Many Chinese monks traveled extensively for their education, visiting such famous mountain temples and sometimes remaining in one to study and serve for several years. In China and Japan the cries of wild monkeys are thought poignant because of their resemblance to the sounds of the human voice.

A Chance Verse

In my leftover years I've somehow stumbled and lost my way,
Unheeding let seasons of light and shade slip through my
    dreams.
In all the world there's no fool so great as I —
How much bitterness against myself is still in my thoughts!

Ryūshū Shūtaku

Ryūshū Shūtaku (1308–88) was a disciple of Musō Sōseki (1275–1351). It was Musō whose influence first with Go-Daigo and then with the Ashikaga generals and the imperial protegés they sponsored in rivalry against his party brought Zen as an institution to the peak of its public prosperity. Musō has been variously depicted as a clever busybody and as a recluse brought unwillingly into the arena of official life; among his good works was the founding of the Tenryūji, which he persuaded the Ashikaga to endow for the welfare of Go-Daigo's soul after the latter's death in exile. (Like so many of his contemporaries, Musō trained for a time under Issan Ichinei, but he seems to have found Issan's instruction puzzling. The relationship was brief and unsatisfactory.) Musō possessed artistic as well as practical gifts. The gardens that he designed are celebrated; he believed that if — but only if — designing a garden was approached in the proper spirit, the work became a religious exercise. Musō had no gift for poetry, however, although he wrote quantities of verse like everyone else, and he had little sympathy for would-be poets. He railed against monks who were preoccupied with literary pursuits, calling them unfit for religious life. Nevertheless, many of the best poets of the *gozan* were among his disciples. Ryūshū is the first of five represented in this volume.

Ryūshū was a devotee of Esoteric Buddhism as well as Zen. He worshiped the cult figures Fudō and Jizō and was vouchsafed supernatural experiences. Under the name of Myōtaku he became known as a painter of images of Fudō. Gidō Shūshin praised his prescriptions for frugal living. No fewer than nine of Musō's disciples (as well as Musō himself) received the title of Kokushi, Preceptor to the Nation; Ryūshū was offered it but refused.

Sweeping Leaves

Having no coins to buy firewood
I sweep up leaves that have fallen in the lane.
Each leaf is precious, a fragment of yellow gold;
The mounds are lovely as red brocade.
I scold myself: squanderer, to crave warmth for my knees —
Rather I'd soothe the coldness in my breast.
Returning from my rounds I sit by the lighted hearth
And listen again to the trickle of rain on the steps.

At Night on a Journey

Bell-sounds night after night — falling on whose ears?
The traveler's dream: forty years pass in an instant:
Sitting up by shutters under the pines, I forget "I" —
Clouds issue from the peaks; the moon courses the heavens.

The second line refers to a Chinese folktale that became popular in Japan. A man who has come to the capital to seek his fortune lies down for a nap and experiences in dream all the vicissitudes of a long, glorious but ultimately tragic official career; awaking, he discovers that no more time has passed than it has taken for his supper of yellow millet to cook.

Tesshū Tokusai

A landscape painter as well as a poet, Tesshū Tokusai visited China and received a title of honor from the Yuan court. Upon returning to Japan he became a follower of Musō Sōseki at the Tenryūji. His exact dates are not known.

Lament for Myself

Old country monk that I am, I'm ignorant of the seasons —
But how should I fathom so paltry a thing as the passing of
   months and days?
Fame and profit, right and wrong, I've long since forgotten —
Lotus-leaf clothing, pine seeds for food just come from my
   karma.

Living in the Mountains

To be purged of the dust of striving among men
In the pure robes of meditation I sit on the green moss.
In my west window the setting sun, autumn darkening —
Falling leaves scatter down upon the stone pedestals.

This was a favorite subject for Tesshū, and he wrote a number of poems that bear
this title. The second line is a variation on one from a series of poems with this
title by the poet-monk Kuan-hsiu (d. early tenth century): "In the pure robes of
meditation I sit on the green banks."

Gidō Shūshin

Gidō Shūshin (1325–88) became dharma-disciple to Musō Sōseki in his seventeenth year; after Musō's death he became leader of the late master's lineage. In his eighteenth year he wanted to visit the continent but was prevented by illness and made no further attempts. His relations with the military government seem to have begun in 1359, when he was invited to Kamakura by Ashikaga Motouji, Shogunal Deputy for the East and younger brother of the shogun Yoshiakira. In 1380 he was summoned to Kyoto by Motouji's nephew, the young shogun Ashikaga Yoshimitsu, whose confidante and adviser he became. (An account of the relations between the two men, based on Gidō's diary, appears in Sir George Sansom, *A History of Japan, 1334–1615* [Stanford: Stanford University Press, 1961], 161–66.) Warm and gentle by nature, genuinely, stubbornly modest, Gidō was reluctant to give up his relative seclusion in order to participate in official life, but the relationship between the older and the younger man seems nevertheless to have been trusting and affectionate. Gidō expounded Confucian precepts to Yoshimitsu; as the shogun's interest turned toward Zen, Gidō instructed him in meditation.

When the shogun visited the monk's residence, the entertainment often included one of Gidō's favorite pastimes, the composition of *renku*, linked verse in which Chinese couplets alternated with Japanese hemistiches; a frequent participant was Nijō Yoshimoto, who occupies an important place in the history of poetry in Japanese as codifier of the rules for *renga*. There were also Chinese poetry contests, in which Gidō took part. Perhaps it was the intensity of his own passion for Chinese poetry that caused Gidō to warn his disciples repeatedly that literary pursuits must never be more than a diversion and to quote them Musō's adjurations.

Gidō lectured on the *San-t'i Shih*. In his twenty-third year he had made an anthology of a thousand poems by Chinese Zen monks of Sung and Yuan times, entitled *Jōwashū*. The manuscript was lost in a fire; some three decades later, while resting at the hot springs at Arima during his final illness, he reconstructed it — he claimed in fact not to be really ill but to have retired to Arima solely for this purpose. Three weeks before his death he entrusted the manuscript to Zekkai Chūshin, charging him to have it engraved for printing. Preface and afterword to the collection of Gidō's own poems were written by Chūgan Engetsu. Of all the *gozan* poets, Gidō was the most prolific. He had the satisfaction of hearing that his poems were praised in China.

In the Morning of the Year Written to Discourage Guests

This New Year will have its months and days, all perfectly
    ordinary —
But the whole world makes a fuss now, bringing wishes of the
    season;
When an old man meets the spring he'd rather just have his
    sleep:
Don't come; don't wake me from my afternoon doze.

In Asia, as in the West until recent centuries, the New Year began with spring.

The Bamboo Sparrow

Doesn't peck up millet from the government storehouse,
Doesn't bore holes through the master's house;
It dwells a lifetime in the mountain groves
And roosts at nightfall on a branch of bamboo.

"Who can say the sparrow has no horn? How else could it bore through my house?" From the *Book of Odes* (Legge, *The Chinese Classics*, vol. 4, 27).

Improvisation upon Leaving the Nanzenji to Go into Retirement

Vast sea of pain; waves cling to the sky!
Eight winds of passion drive my leaking boat.
Though I've others yet to rescue, I'll first pole for the nearer
    shore,
To drift as of old in the shallows, by the banks among
    flowering reeds.

The Buddhists make "ferrying across" their metaphor for salvation. The leaking boat is the poet's own self, still possessed of the *āśravas,* leaks or "outflows" from the sense organs, and hence confined to the stream of transmigration by the passions.

Gidō became abbot of the highest-ranking *gozan* monastery, the Nanzenji, early in 1385, only after repeatedly attempting to decline the honor. When in the autumn of 1386 he wished to retire from his post, the monks, inconsolable, refused to allow the beating of the drum that would summon them to receive the announcement of his departure.

Camellia Blossoms

My ancient hut's a ruin, half-hidden under moss —
Who'd have his carriage pause before my gate?
But my servant boy understands that I've beckoned an
    honored guest,
For he leaves unswept the camellia blossoms that fill the
    ground.

The Painted Fan

Dim fringe of cloud and lustrous moon-disc:
The little boats have left for harbor; now is dusk.
Surely the fishers need not fear that their homes may be hard
to find:
Village under plum blossoms radiant at river's edge.

A great many poems describing scenes in paintings are included in the anthology of Gidō's works; the poet evidently took particular delight in these.

Landscapes on the Two Faces of a Fan

In the mist-rimmed pine grove a temple —
Amid willows at water's edge the huts of fishermen —
The monk, content with empty bowl, lets noon pass;
Fishermen spread their nets to dry under a slanting sun.

This poem is in an unusual variant of the *chüeh-chü* form, with six (rather than five or seven) characters to each line.

On a Picture of a Cat

The kitten asleep by his mother's side
Already possesses the knight's blood-oath spirit:
A word to you, mice: you fellows should know
That truly it's said "A youth deserves respect!"

The quotation in the last line is from the Confucian *Analects* 9.22. "The Master said, 'A youth is to be regarded with respect. How do we know that his future will not be equal to our present?'" (Legge, *The Chinese Classics,*, vol. 1, 223). This poem is in the same form as the preceding.

Instruction for My Disciples
on the Eighth Day of the Twelfth Month

As age draws on it's not easy to achieve the Way,
Sickness may make it hard to go forth from the cloister —
But how else can all sentient beings be saved?
Yet greater are the sufferings on the paths of this world.
He awakes from sleep; a star hangs low over his door;
As the skies grow bright, snow covers the mountain passes.
I pity him from afar, the old man with whorls of kinky hair
Who barefoot descends the towering slopes.

According to one tradition, on this day, having achieved enlightenment in the hours before dawn, Śākyamuni set out from the Himalayas, where for six years he had meditated. In Zen temples the anniversary was one of many during the year that were celebrated with a formal sermon by the abbot. Whorls of hair curled to the right were one of the thirty-two major marks of a Buddha. The scene has often been represented in painting.

Written for Amusement during His Illness to Instruct His Pupils

The hundred fleshly diseases afflict the yet-tainted self —
A remnant, this lingering life: already I'm neighbor to the
    spirits.
Rather I'd laugh at you, my foolish disciples,
Who would grasp the empty blossoms, keep spring from its
    passing.

Kūge, Gidō's pen name as poet, means literally "empty blossoms" — a Buddhist
metaphor for the too-soon-fading phenomena of the world of illusion.

Hymn for Offering Incense upon the Buddha's Attainment of the Path

The morning star returns night after night;
The snows of the twelfth month linger from year to year.
Silly:
Gautama's achieving some "special" state;
Looking for a knife in the water by marks in the ship's hull.

Guchū Shūkyū

Guchū Shūkyū (1323–1409) had his first interview with Musō Sōseki in his thirteenth year; Musō made him the pupil of his own nephew and chief disciple, Shun'ya Myōha (1311–88). Another teacher of Guchū's youth was Ryūshū Shūtaku. In 1341 Guchū went to China, returning in 1351 in time to see Musō, who died not long afterward. Guchū remained by his grave for three years, living alone.

Guchū was adviser to Yoshimitsu's successor, Yoshimochi, occupying a position much like that which Gidō had held with the earlier shogun. There is a story that Guchū received a sword wound in the forehead at the hands of a Nanzenji monk who doubted the genuineness of the religious inheritance he claimed to have received from his master in China, and that because of it he went to live in seclusion; later he honored the grave of his attacker, without whom, he said, he would never have experienced the joy of solitary meditation.

Matching the Rhymes of "Weeping over the Death of a Child by Drowning" (another's poem)

A child swallows water, tumbles, and is given to the deep current.
Don't speak of his father and mother — even the demons would mourn!
Though they summoned his precious five-year-old soul it didn't come back:
Frail as the dew on the grave he lies buried at the roots of the grasses.

Refusing Guests

One in black robes who feared the approach of his
    black-robed fellows
Would be just like a man of Ch'in who didn't love Ch'in.
Though I don't know all about the Pure Land, my heart
    instinctively knows it's there —
This world's true pleasures are in being alone and poor.

Buddhist monks in China and Japan dressed in black. Belief in the Pure Land of
Bliss, the paradise in the West created by the Buddha Amida for those who
meditate on him or invoke his name, is almost universal in Mahayana Buddhism;
Amidist devotions became popular in the *gozan* monasteries toward the end of
the fourteenth century.

Listening to the Rain
on the Second Night of the Third Month

Tinkling belt-pendants sound beyond the bamboo:
What fine young gentleman has come into the mountains?
Tonight, I strain my ears, imagining —
Tomorrow, peach blossoms open on a thousand trees.

Zekkai Chūshin

Zekkai Chūshin (1336–1405) became Musō's disciple at the Tenryūji in 1348 and, like Guchū, studied under Shun'ya; he also studied with Ryūzan Tokken (1284–1358), whom historians pair with Sesson as a bringer of firsthand knowledge of China. In 1364 he left Kyoto to live in Kamakura among Gidō's followers. In 1368, the year of the founding of the Ming, he went to China, remaining until 1376. His pilgrimage is important especially because it took place at a time when new missionaries were no longer coming to Japan. Zekkai enjoyed the favor of Gidō's shogunal patrons, the shogun Yoshimitsu and the shogunal deputy Motouji, and later of Yoshimitsu's successor, Yoshimochi. Because of his facility in writing the parallel prose used for elegant state documents, he was chosen to compose the letter that Yoshimitsu sent in 1401 to the Yung-lo emperor (but the letter ultimately proved to be a source of humiliation, for it was criticized by rivals as injurious to the national dignity). On another occasion he was sent as emissary to remonstrate with a rebellious vassal. Zekkai, excitable and emotional, opposed his Ashikaga masters on occasion, and several times fled them into retirement.

After Gidō's death, Zekkai succeeded him as leader of Musō's school. Gidō and Zekkai are called the "two jewels" of *gozan bungaku*. Of all the *gozan* poets it is undeniably Zekkai who is the most accomplished, whose poems are consistently sustained compositions rather than collections of brilliant couplets. A Ming monk wrote preface and afterword to the anthology of his writings, and among the men who praised them for the purity of their Chinese was Sung Ching-lien (1310–81, also called Sung Lien). The seeds of the decline of *gozan bungaku* can be seen in

Zekkai's work. His subject matter is entirely secular; long verses are architectonically constructed of learned allusions. His willingness to put his literary talents to the service of the government portends a time when *gozan* monks will abandon religion to become clerks.

All of his poems in the present selection were written in China.

An Old Temple

Which way did it face? this ancient temple gate,
Wisteria vines deep on all four walls.
Flowers near the eaves lie crushed after the rains;
Wild birds sing for the visitor alone;
Grass engulfs the seat of the World-Honored One,
And from its base has melted the patron's gold.
These broken tablets show no years or months —
Hard to tell whether they're from T'ang or Sung.

Ascending a High Building after Rain

Passing showers have filled the sky and washed the new
    autumn;
With my friend hand-in-hand I climb the tower above the
    river,
Wishing a remembrance of Chung-hsüan's ancient regret —
In the broken mist and scattered trees, my unendurable
    sorrow.

Chung-hsüan was the *tz'u*, "style," of Wang Ts'an (A.D. 177–217), whose famous
Teng-lou fu ("Essay in Rhyme on Ascending the Tower") expressed his homesick-
ness for Ch'ang-an.

Mist on the River

The single band of the river's flow steeps heaven in coolness,
Distant and nearby peaks have merged in the autumn mist;
It seems with green gauze they'd bar men's view —
The queens of the water, too modest to show their lovely
    selves.

The "queens of the water" are the two daughters of the legendary emperor Yao
who became consorts of his successor Shun and drowned themselves after the
latter's death. They were popularly venerated as goddesses of the Hsiang River.

Recording My Longings at the Beginning of Autumn

At the first cries of wild geese from borderland, evening dew
    thickens:
The wayfarer feels yet again how the years have gone by —
Once a summons to An-chi was entrusted to a crane;
Though centuries pass, Hsü Fu's boat has not returned.
In southern mountains the purple-beans lie wasted in the long
    rains;
By northern lakes the red lotuses have shed their blooms in
    the clear autumn.
Fond you may be of tours, but they make a man age:
Chi-tzu, cease your aversion for your five-acre field!

Line 1: Dew so heavy and extensive that the fields appear white characterizes the
north Chinese autumn.

Lines 3–4: An-chi Sheng was a Taoist magician who claimed to have the secret
of immortality. The First Emperor of the Ch'in talked with him for three days
and nights, but he refused to divulge it and departed, telling the emperor to
send for him in the islands of the immortals in the eastern sea. The emperor
despatched Hsü Fu with 3,000 youths and maidens to bear him a letter (an
imperial summons to a Taoist adept, called a "crane-letter") and bring back the
herbs of immortality. The legend is that Hsü Fu went to Japan, where he yet
remains.

Line 8: Chi-tzu was the *tz'u* of Su Ch'in, the minister who forged the so-called
vertical alliance of six states during the Warring States period. He had once been
poor, scorned even by his relatives for traveling in search of employment, but
after attaining power he returned to his village and said: "If you would have me
be wealthy with a five-acre field near the capital, what do you think of my
possessing the ministerial seals of six states?"

Rhyme Describing the Three Mountains, Composed in Response to the Imperial Command

Before Kumano's peak is Hsü Fu's shrine,
The mountains are rich with herbs grown lush after rain,
And now upon the sea the billowing waves are calm:
Kind winds a myriad miles will speed him home.

During his visit to China, Zekkai was called before Emperor T'ai-tsu of the Ming and questioned about his homeland — in particular, about the site in Kumano where Hsü Fu was said to be buried. Zekkai responded with a poem in which the calm sea is made to symbolize the tranquility of T'ai-tsu's reign, so benign that Hsü Fu will at long last return to China with his precious cargo. The "Three Mountains" of the title are, of course, Japan (see p. 45).

Chūjo Joshin

Chūjo Joshin accompanied Zekkai to China but was prevented by illness from returning with him. The dates of his birth and death are unknown.

On Falling Ill

As spring waned I fell ill; now autumn approaches.
In my bedchamber the year's lights and shadows flow like
    water.
Willow catkins and peach blossoms have become yesterday's
    dream;
Wu-t'ung trees and crickets excite fresh grief —
Sickness has many kinds but all alike are of man's nature;
Though a life be blessed with a hundred years, it must yet
    cease.
At noon and evening when cool winds arise from the ends of
    heaven,
Worn clean as I am, I wish a moment to climb alone the
    storied pavilion.

Gakuin Ekatsu

Zekkai's disciple Gakuin Ekatsu (1367–1425) toured Zen monasteries in China from 1386 to 1394. After his return to Japan he lived for a time in a hermitage in Tosa Province on the island of Shikoku, devoting himself to poetry. It was he who compiled the anthology of Zekkai's poetry. Gakuin was posthumously given the title of Kokushi.

The Sound of Heating Water for Tea

Faint singing: in a distant valley wind arises in the pines.
Full boiling: on the cold river the first spring rains fall.
In the daytime bustle of a city temple the heart grows fuddled
    as with drink:
To hear the pure sound with unsullied mind late at night I
    boil water for tea.

Detaining a Visitor on a Chilly Night

A moment's brilliance, flower of the lamp, deeply lights the
  snow;
With happy face I hasten to greet you at the shuttered
  window:
Since last we parted it's been colder in my heart than steel —
I listen to the end, as the bells of Ch'ang-an strike midnight.

Visiting the Rozanji in Late Autumn

The mountain temple stands bleak in the afternoon:
It's autumn, time of yellowing, falling leaves.
Guests pass by but the tea-hearth is silent;
Monks dwell here but their chambers are dark behind clumps
   of bamboo.
Rozan's peak surges into view from the corner where I sit;
A southland valley river floats past my veranda.
   What of all this most moves me?
Brocade-bright maple leaves washed in the pure stream.

The Rozanji was founded in 938 and moved in 1245 to Funaokayama, a hill with
a fine view in the northern part of Kyoto. (It is now in the Kyoto flatlands, not
far from the old imperial palace.) Lu-shan, for which the temple was named
(Rozan is the Japanese reading of the characters), is a scenic area in Kiangsi that is
the site of numerous temples. It has been suggested that the river of this poem
may be the Kamiyagawa, a small tributary of the Kamo River that arises in
present-day Funaokayama Park.

Ichū Tsūjo

Ichū Tsūjo (1349–1429) was a scholar and persuasive evangelist who lived and worked chiefly in the great Kyoto monasteries, in his old age retiring into seclusion. He never visited China.

Sent to a Friend

From the river lotuses, fragrance drifts on the air;
Evening rains echo in the clear autumn.
Swans take their nightly rest in pairs
And again fly up, pass on to their separate provinces:
So soon after parting, you're a thousand miles away —
So far a distance, that no letter comes —
Insensate, the waters of the river
That day after day come with the swelling tide!

Evening Rain by the Bridge

Showering, the rain by the bridge,
Under shadow, at nightfall is not yet hushed.
A fisherman in straw coat waits hesitant on the bluff;
The monks' gong sounds across the central stream.
Sad and still, bush clover at twilight —
Blue into the distance, water oats in autumn.
How beautiful is the clear shallow water!
Tranquil: a single sand gull.

About a Painting

Two old fishermen on the riverbank in spring,
Their boats made fast, walk on the soft sand.
They've started to chat — whatever about?
They're planning to go see the plum trees in bloom.

Bibliographical Note

The following is a list of works that have furnished texts for the poems (followed by the abbreviations used in the Finding List) or that I have found particularly helpful in preparing the introduction and brief biographies. The reader should be warned that the biographies are based in large part on secondary literature; I have consulted primary sources in a number of cases but have not done so consistently and do not cite them as individual titles.

Akamatsu Toshihide, ed. *Nihon Bukkyō Shi: Chūsei Hen.* (1967).

Haga Kōshirō. "Zensō no Bungakukan no Hensen." *Nihon Koten Bungaku Taikei Geppō* series 2, number 23 (February 1966), 6–8.

Imaeda Aishin. *Zenshū no Rekishi.* 1962.

Kamimura Kankō, ed. *Gozan Bungaku Zenshū.* 5 vols. 1936 (abbreviated *Zenshū*).

Kitamura Sawakichi. *Gozan Bungaku Shikō.* 1941.

Mori Tadashige. *Waka Shika Sakka Jiten.* 1972.

Ogata Korekiyo. *Nihon Kanbungakushi Kōgi.* 1961.

Okada Masayuki. *Nihon Kanbungaku Shi.* 1954.

Tamamura Takeji. *Gozan Bungaku.* 1966.

———. *Gozan Bungaku Shinshū.* 6 vols. 1967–72 (abbreviated *Shinshū*).

———. *Musō Kokushi.* 1958.

Tsuji Zennosuke, ed. *Kūge Nichiyō Kūfu Ryakushū.* 1939.

———. "Musō Kokushi." *Shigaku Zasshi* 27 (1918), 429–58.

———. *Nihon Bukkyō Shi* 4. 1960.

Washio Junkei. *Nihon Bukka Jinmei Jisho.* 1917.

Yamagishi Tokuhei, ed. *Gozan Bungaku Shū — Edo Kanshi Shū* (*Nihon Koten Bungaku Taikei* 89). 1968 (abbreviated *NKBT*).

Finding List

For poems that appear in *NKBT* no further citation is given except in special cases.

A NOTE ABOUT THE AUTHOR

Marian Ury is Professor of Comparative Literature at the University of California, Davis. Her publications include *Tales of Times Now Past* (University of California Press, 1979) and numerous articles and book reviews.

Printed and bound by CPI Group (UK) Ltd, Croydon, CR0 4YY

27/03/2025

14649112-0001